# This book belongs to:

# Tips *and* Tricks

1. Spend precious time as you color these detailed hedgehog images for you and easy ones for your grandchild.

2. Designed as a positive experience for your grandchild as they color and learn!

3. Portrait and landscape images: on one side of the page to allow for the use of markers, colored pencils, gel pens, or crayons.

4. *Bonus: vocabulary words found in the curriculum of all elementary classrooms.

5. Develop or review small motor skills with these adorable hedgehog coloring illustrations.

# Bonus Hedgehog Vocabulary Words

**habitat**-place where a plant or an animal lives and grows

**hibernate**-animals who spend the winter sleeping

**senses**-sight, smell, hearing, taste, and touch

**mammal**-a warm-blooded animal with a backbone

**species**-animals or plants with the same characteristics

**nocturnal**-active and appearing at night

**predator**-animals that hunt other animals for food

**climate**-the average weather conditions of an area

**domesticated**-an animal trained to live with people (as a pet)

**adaptation**-parts of an animal to help them survive

A baby hedgehog is called a HOG-LET. The male is called a "BOAR" and a "SOW" for the female.

One to seven HOG-LETS are usually born in a litter.

The hedgehog's HABITAT is the edge of woodlands, grasslands, gardens, meadows, and even parks!

They don't have very good eye-site, so they use their SENSES (smell and hearing) to help them find food.

These adorable MAMMALS weigh 14 TO 39 ounces (1 kilogram).

They are 5 to 12 inches long (13 to 30 cm), the length of a teaspoon!

Hedgehogs can walk six miles (10 kilometers) per hour! That's faster than a child!

There are fifteen different SPECIES of hedgehogs.

Hedgehogs have approximately 5,000 to 7,000 spines, which drop off after a year, and a new spine grows.

These NOCTURNAL creatures usually come out at night, but sometimes appear after it rains!

HEDGEHOGS live all over the WORLD, but most of the population is in Europe, Asia, and Africa.

These delightful ground creatures can swim, climb trees, fences, and rock walls!

They snuffle through hedges and undergrowth for insects, but they also eat mice, snails, lizards, frogs, eggs, and even snakes!

These carnivores know how to take down a snake and eat it, too! They are immune to the venom of most snakes.

Hedgehogs also enjoy eating berries and fruit when they're abundant in the autumn.

As it searches for food, it makes pig-like grunts.
That's how they got the name hedgehogs!

Hedgehogs snuffle, snort, and even hiss if they feel threatened!

They can curl up into a spiny ball to protect their head, legs, and tail.

Hedgehog ADAPTATIONS such as their thick, spiny coats protect them from PREDATORS such as the fox and badgers.

Here's a hedgehog secret: they eat poisonous plants, then lick their spines, which hides their scent from PREDATORS!

In places such as Northern Europe, hedgehogs HIBERNATE throughout the winter.

Those living in warmer CLIMATES will hibernate during the extreme heat and drought.

Even during HIBERNATION, hedgehogs have been known to appear during the day for sunshine, water, and food.

Those living in moderate climates are active throughout the year.

HEDGEHOGS used to be called "URCHINS" which inspired the name of similar spiky sea creatures.

These adorable creatures have been called
"HEDGE-PIGS" and "URCHINS" in books by
famous authors such as William Shakespeare.

The average hedgehog lives to seven years old.

A DOMESTICATED hedgehog can live to almost 15 years old.

# Draw and color your hedgehog.

Draw and color your hedgehog.

# Grandma _and_ Me!

## Super Cool Hedgehog Facts
## Vocabulary Words
## & Coloring Book!

by florabella publishing

Thank you for your recent purchase.
We hope you've enjoyed your
Grandma and Me!
Super Cool Hedgehog Facts,
Vocabulary Words, and Coloring Book!

*If you love hedgehogs as much as we do, please see
our Super Cool Hedgehog Activity Book
by florabella publishing!

www.ingramcontent.com/pod-product-compliance
Lightning Source LLC
Chambersburg PA
CBHW081848250726
48659CB00008B/2647